KNITTING FOR BEGINNERS:

The guide on how to learn knitting using pictures, illustrations and easy patterns to create amazing projects

Madeline Stitch

TABLE OF CONTENTS

Introduction

I am welcoming you to an exciting journey that is set to ignite your world of passion and creativity. Knitting emanates from the word 'knot.' The fascinating part is that you can dramatically modify the look and drape of a stitch pattern by changing yarn and sizes of needles.

According to research, the first form of clothing that was made, which is similar to knitting was socks. These were crafted using a method called 'Nalebinding,' which makes use of a single needle and thread.

Over the years, with the grasp of creativity and innovating ideas, knitting has tremendously blossomed to not just being a craft but a channel for earning. Various knitting designs and patterns have also evolved.

This book will expose you to the knowledge and ideas that you need to kick start in your world of knitting. It would help you to know how and where to start from in the knitting process; making yarns, needles, casting/binding on, purling, etc.

As you practice the guideline here, you will be equipped to explore intricate styles that exist. As well as become open to creative ideas that will expand your horizon.

Get acquainted with the walkthrough process that has been illustrated with pictures and start knitting today.

Knitting is a method by which long needles interlink a series of loops made from one continuous thread or knot. Loop or knot binds to another, resulting in a flat piece of material called a cloth when there were enough loops. A textile is a cloth created by interlacing natural fibers, such as wool or cotton, or synthetic fibers, such as polyester, to cover another simple meaning. Many textiles are produced either by knitting or by a process called weaving, which interlaces vertical and horizontal threads on a device called a loom. Knitted goods tend to be more elastic and deliver more than woven fabrics, which tend to be thicker and firmer. Knitting has been around for quite a long time. Scholars think this might have been invented in the Middle East in the 5th century BC, and then spread to other parts of the world. Knitting can be performed either by hand or by a knitting machine, which uses many needles of steel mounted on a frame called a needle bar.

Knitting is the process which produces cloth from thread. It's used to create garments, toys, home wares and all sorts of exciting things! It's a skill that can be enjoyed by anyone – and it's growing in popularity every single day with celebrities such as Sarah Jessica Parker and Cameron Diaz happily declaring their love for the hobby. But, it's actually so much more than that. Knitting can be beneficial to your health! It has been proven to lower blood pressure, relax the enthusiast and even burn calories (approximately 55 for half an hour of knitting).

In fact, knitting has become so popular that there are now many competitions and challenges associated with it. Let us now move on to the real definition and tutorial on how to knit.

Chapter 1 Brief History of Knitting

The Historian Richard Rutt moderately recommends that knitting started in Egypt somewhere in the range of 500 and 1200 A.D.

A private researcher, Rudolf Pfister, discovered some of the knitted fabric of East Syria. A few specialists then contended over the Dura sections, and have been demonstrated to be a result of nalbinding.

Nalbinding is a knotless texture creation system that originates before knitting. This sort of movement utilizes a solitary needle to tie and combine fabrics, while knitting utilizes a couple of needles and a yarn to make circles. It was rehearsed by the Coptic Christians in Egypt during the fourth century to make a couple of Coptic socks – a generally formed piece of clothing to fit the foot for thongs or shoes. It was likewise utilized by the Scandinavians who live in cold, rocky districts to create extra-warm caps, gloves, and head garments in the last 50% of the first century. Rutt unequivocally accepts that the art of knitting may have been imagined by the Egyptians to spare time and vitality in making their garments. Contrasted with knitting, nail-restricting expends additional time and requires extraordinary finesse. Be that as it may, this texture delivers a smoother, denser, and more sturdy texture than knitting.

An authentic knitted piece has been found in Egypt, around 1000-1400 A.D... Made using white and indigo cotton, its intricacy in configuration solidly shows that this thing isn't the absolute originally knitted thing that has been delivered.

Century in Europe: Madonna Knitting

In Spain, the Arabs introduced the practice of knitting. It was used to make formal clothing and extras by the Catholic Church. Among the most punctual knitted artful culminations were two Arab-knit silk cushions that were found in the famous tombs of a religious community in northern Spain, dated in the eleventh century.

During the fourteenth century, this action, in the long run, arrived at the remainder of Europe. It got one of crafted by the exceptionally gifted craftsmen. Knitting societies were built up in France in 1268, and to pick up enrollment, one must breeze through every one of the assessments to be given to them. With the utilization of beautiful yarns stitched with brilliant strings, these artisans have made gloves, cushions, and relic handbags for the holy people. They additionally knitted stockings, pouches, sleeves, girdles, and drawstring bags known as "jabs" (Nargi).

The sixteenth Century: Knitting in the United Kingdom

The purl stitch technique was created in the sixteenth century by the English knitters. It was utilized to knit stockings, a sort of volume of clothing that was advanced as an incredible fashion pattern for the Italian and Spanish men. Ruler Henry VIII was the central British sovereignty to wear knitted stockings. It filled in as the pants of today, setting up an exquisite, fashionable look. Because of the appeal of this thing, Queen Elizabeth I, the little girl of King Henry the VIII, supported the development of knitting societies. She additionally started utilizing knit silk stockings and elaborate knitted sleeves for her outfits during her rule.

Various particular styles in knitting likewise showed up in the British Isles. One of these is the cabling of a sailor's knitted sweater called the Gansey.

The Rise of Technology in the Art of Knitting

The world of knitting inevitably created and extended as an exchange. It was gone through countries by the European pilgrims and settlers during the mechanical upset. It was in 1589 that a machine for knitting was created. The Englishman William Lee made the stocking outline or the knitting machine, the first historically speaking gadget that mirrors the hand developments of a knitter. It has 8 needles to the inch and just delivers a coarse texture. Then on, Lee improved the instrument with 20 needles to the inch and had the option to knit stockings with silk and wool.

A few urban communities like Nottingham turned into a significant maker of machine-knitted fabrics. The place that is known for Leicestershire and a portion of its neighboring nations additionally wandered in hosiery or the legwear industry. With the growing number of requests in the market, the knitting machine makers additionally expanded in the generation, yet in addition to the advancement of the various sorts of machinery, for example, the round knitting machine.

Knitting as a Voice for Nationalism

During the Revolutionary war, the youthful and old assembled to sew and knit, as they show support for the nationalists. The individuals knit their very own garments to blacklist British merchandise, indicating their confidence and autonomy from the British. Martha Washington, George Washington's significant other, is additionally a committed knitter. She gathered the spouses of the high-positioning authorities in the pilgrim armed force to sew and repair garments, for example, socks and outfits for the soldiers.

Knitting and its Road to Fashion

During the 1920s, knit wears, for example, sweaters and pullovers assumed a primary job in the world of fashion. It turned into a fashion articulation for the two people everything being equal. It had been related to sports and relaxation, for example, golf, tennis and cricket. Coco Chanel additionally grasped this art, utilizing such things and patterns. On the extraordinary sadness, the unmistakable quality of knitting proceeded with its adventure, yet, changed its way as a method for need. Since it was a lot less expensive to make your very own garments, individuals favored creating their very own as opposed to purchasing the business items.

The engineered yarn and strands were presented in the 1950s, making it more straightforward for the mass to deliver their knits. Carefully assembled knitting turned into a method for leisure activity as the knitting machines got widespread in the market, creating prepared-to-wear things and garments at a quicker speed. Smaller than regular skirts, sweaters, and dresses made of strands soared its notoriety 10 years after.

Today's World of Knitting

With the headway of technology, some PC programs gave more accommodation to knitters. The utilization of web-based life likewise had a unique influence on commercializing this craft. The web enables us to interface and offer interests with different knitters around the globe using some knitting circle destinations. Instructional recordings and podcasts are likewise accessible, giving comfort to the individuals who are eager to learn about this type of art.

Chapter 2 What Are The Benefits Of Knitting?

There are several physical and health benefits of knitting for both adults and children. Some of them are explained below:

- Stress reduction: The rhythmic and repetitive motions that are done when knitting helps us to relax. According to the results of a study conducted by Dr. Barry Jacobs of Prince town University, repetitive motions performed by animals activate the release of serotonin, which is a neurotransmitter that is responsible for calmness and well-being. Also, Betsan Corkhill, an English physiotherapist, reported that as her patients engaged in knitting, some of them who were sluggish, stressed, and depressed became better. Knitting helped them to manage destructive thoughts and behaviors. Therefore, knitting helps to reduce and manage stress.

- Prevention of several diseases: The results of several studies have revealed that knitting helps to prevent such conditions as arthritis, tendinitis, cognitive decline, Parkinson's, anxiety, among others. Also, knitting stimulates the entire brain at once, and this improves the proper functioning of the brain.

- Helps to improve concentration: Knitting helps both adults and kids to tone down hyperactivity and improve concentration. It helps people to learn to stay in the present moment. Also, the fact that as you knit, you see the result immediately helps to reinforce your ability to concentrate.

• Can be a stream of income: even though you can begin knitting as a cheap hobby, it can turn out to be a reliable stream of income. You can make fabrics and sell them to the people around you. Also, you can make clothes for yourself, thereby reducing the percentage of your income spent on purchasing clothes.

• Boosts your self-esteem: Knitting is about creativity. In other words, when you knit, you bring into reality what was not formerly in existence. And when this is done, it boosts your self-esteem. You become more confident in your creative ability. The ripple effect is that you no longer demonstrate the inferiority complex.

Very many people crochet to pass the time. If you are in this category, you should know that you are doing yourself a lot of good. Not only does the time you spend making several designs help you to reduce accumulated body stress and anxiety, but it also helps you to:

1. Feel fulfilled. You get to give yourself a pat on the back when you are done with a particular project. Imagine creating something from just a hook and yarn?

2. Relieve depression: now, there is something creative and constructive that you are thinking about. You will have less or no time for destructive and depressive thoughts. It has been proved that doing something you like doing makes the brain to secrete

hormones such as dopamine and serotonin. Dopamine works like an anti-depressant, making you feel good.

Be happy: Crochet works when well-done are very beautiful. You'll be happy to be the brain behind a beautiful piece of artwork.

3.   You might make an extra income from it. Especially in climes where people have to work two or three jobs to make ends meet, selling beautiful crochet pieces might be a source of income for the crocheter.

4.   Slow down or prevent memory loss altogether: memory loss can be slowed down when one partakes in logical exercises, such as crochet.

Also, it helps you to develop fine motor skills. People who have arthritis might do well to consider picking up crocheting as a hobby. It will help to keep their fingers nimble. The craft of crocheting will make you more patient. There is no rushing it really, it can only be done with the hands, so it will help you in learning that some things take time. Working on stitches over time will also help you to have a sense of focus and pay attention to detail. Not paying attention to detail might lead to frogging.

The list is almost endless actually but let's focus more on the bone of contention – what do you need to crochet successfully?

Clicking ceaselessly with a couple of needles and some yarn has benefits that work out positively past something new to wear. Get some answers concerning the wellbeing and social advantages of knitting.

Knitting is useful for the mind

The focus required to follow a pattern and monitor which yarn (or even which needles) we're utilizing, ascertaining how much yarn is required, including lines and columns, in addition to learning new abilities as we ace new join and new patterns... the total of what this has been appeared to help fight off gentle intellectual debilitation, the decrease in the intensity of observation: thinking, thinking and recollecting.

Furthermore, knitting benefits the two sides of the mind: directly for innovativeness, left for rationale and math's.

Knitting is agreeable

It very well may be, if you consolidate knitting with seeing companions. What's more, that is effortlessly done as knitting is convenient so that you can take it with you for evening tea, pints in the bar, or to take a break while voyaging (not on planes, however).

What's more you can join (or start) a knitting gathering, frequently known as a 'fasten and bitch', to visit while you weave, share your work and get tips.

Then there are visits to yarn shops and making appears. Regardless of whether you go alone or with companions, perusing yarn, pack, or being propelled by another person's work can be a genuine friendly exchange.

And afterward there's virtual friendliness employing internet-based life. Following master knitters and planners, seeing companions' most recent works in progress and indicating your own before long cause you to feel some portion of an online network, or get together with remote and have a virtual knitting bunch employing Skye, Zoom or House party.

Knitting keeps you quiet

As the wind on a (presently exhausted) image has it: 'resist the urge to panic and convey yarn'. Also, similar to every single great image, it conveys a relatable truth.

The cadenced, rehashed activities of moving the yarn and the needles and the fixation required to do it right calm the prattle in your psyche. What's more, the more you do it, the better you feel.

As indicated by the Benson-Henry Institute for Mind-Body Medicine at Massachusetts General Hospital, the redundancy of the developments of knitting can inspire the 'unwinding reaction', relating to a bringing down of breathing rate, pulse and circulatory strain.

Knitting is a modest leisure activity

In truth, you'll discover some extortionately evaluated yarns in your nearby haberdashery shop (if you're sufficiently fortunate to have one), however not all things need to be made of cashmere.

You can get a bundle of yarn for several pounds, and needles for less.

Knitting can be a gift

Aside from giving somebody something you've sewn for them, you can likewise pass on your insight.

Training somebody to weave eye to eye is the most ideal approach to learn and demonstrating a companion, youngster or grandkid how to sew is incredible enjoyment, and sets them up with a compensating pastime forever.

Knitting augments your closet

Not exclusively would you be able to make things to wear, however, you can assume the job of style originator, because how these pieces of clothing (or home makes) turn out is heavily influenced by you.

Like the cut yet not the shading? Weave it in your top pick. Also, now and again you needn't bother with a pattern, as with a scarf. Simply cast on, with whatever fleece you need, and prop up until you conclude it's finished.

Knitting supports your confidence

Acing strategies, adhering to a pattern or directions, and finishing an undertaking, and making something that didn't exist before should cause you to feel glad for yourself.

Chapter 3 Understanding Terms and Abbreviation of Knitting

Knitting Terms

Substitute - To work with each other column.

Tie off - To close work by completing with the last column—by knitting two lines; slipping the main join throughout the subsequent fasten; rehashing with every two lines until just one final line remains; and slicing yarn and circling it through the last line.

Cast on - To start by making the primary line, or to include a line or lines—by making a slip circle over the left needle, setting right needle through the circle, ignoring yarn and under the right needle, drawing yarn through the circle, and moving circle to left needle.

Decline - To work less fastens as indicated by guidelines for molding a piece—most ordinarily by a) knitting lines together; or b) slipping a line and disregarding the slipped join while knitting the accompanying line.

Tie Stitch - An example utilizing weave for each line and each line.

Increment - To work extra lines as indicated by directions—most normally by a) making two join from one line by knitting twice into a similar line; b) making two lines from one line by purling twice into a similar line; or c) utilizing the correct needle to get the yarn, place it on the left needle, and sew an extra line into the rear of the new circle made.

Sew - The demonstration, to sew, yet in addition, the most widely recognized line. In designs, sew is curtailed as K and is trailed by the quantity of joins required: K4 = weave four fastens.

Make 1 (see increment) - To work extra lines as per design headings—usually performed to shape a piece; or to make a gap and additionally fasten (for a fancy example), for instance.

Greenery Stitch - The substituting of one sew fasten and one purl join in each line.

Purl - The second most basic join. Though in a weave line you put the correct needle through the line from behind, in the purl fasten you place the correct needle into the front of the left needle join.

Disregard Slipped Stitch — The process involves slipping one fastener (moving the following fastener from left needle to right needle); knitting the corresponding line at that point (yarn underneath then on right needle and yarn got through); slipping line off left needle at that point — so that slipped line and sewed line are now on right needle. The slipped line is eventually raised over and over the weave thread, and off the right needle.

Rehash - To do a similar advance or fasten as just recently educated. On the off chance that the guidelines read [repeat], do a similar activity as you simply did in the step.

Turn around Shaping - The demonstration of working the second side of the piece's shape at the far edge from where it was worked for the principal side. The procedure ordinarily incorporates official off.

Column - The finished arrangement of join worked from one needle to the next, in this manner making it an opportunity to move needles appropriately: from left hand needle in left hand to right hand, and right-hand needle (with push) to left hand.

Selvage (or, selvedge) - Technically meaning crude edge of a piece—the edges that were the first and last columns of join.

Slip - To move a join from left needle to right needle without including yarn.

Stocking Stitch - A fasten design made by substituting one column of weave and one line of purl all through.

Through the Back of the Loop - The demonstration of knitting (or purling) into the rear of the circle on left needle, making a contorted line.

Together-The correct needle (directing left to right) on a knitting column works with the following two joins (or number shown) on the left needle, while the yarn is placed under the right needle, brought over the top, and fastened simultaneously through the two; at that point the two lines are dropped. On a purling board, however, the process the conducted in comparable style with purling activities — right needle is fastened through the front of left needle; and yarn is passed over the highest point of right needle point.

Yarn Back - The activity of putting front-sitting yarn to back, between the two needles.

Yarn Forward - The activity of bringing back-sitting yarn to the front, under the correct needle.

Yarn Front - The demonstration of leaving the effectively front-sitting yarn at the front as opposed to moving it back for a back-sitting yarn join—an activity which will rather make a circle or gap.

Yarn 'Round Needle - The demonstration of going before the following join by folding yarn over the correct needle point (yarn beginning and completing at back for a sew line, yarn beginning and completing at front for a purl line)— in this manner making an opening and an additional line.

Knitting Abbreviations

If you want to start knitting, it is important that you know about knitting abbreviations. Knitting abbreviations are developed to make it easier for hobbyists to follow the instructions of a particular technique.

Major knitting abbreviations are classified according to what they describe. This means that the types of stitch, position of yarn and even the color changes have abbreviations. Below are major knitting abbreviations that you need to know based on their classifications.

Classification	Abbreviations
Side of work	This refers to the work side of the knitted fabric being correct WS: wrong side RS: right side
Types of stitch	K: knit stitch P: purl stitch

	sl st: slip stitch yo: yarn over This K2, P2 means you need to make Knead two stitches together
Scope of stitch	The scope of stitch refers whether the stitches should be knitted together, tog, thus K2tog means that the two stitches should be knitted together. PSS: pass the slipped stitch over PNSO: pass the next stitch over
Orientation of stitch	This refers to the stitches knitted through the back loop. For instance, p2tog tbl means two stitches needed to be purled together through the back loop. KWISE: knitwise PWISE: purlwise
Insertion point of stitch	Insertion point of stitch refers to where you need to insert the next loop to create the stitch. Kb/ K1b: Knit into the row below Pb/ P1b: Purl into the row below P tbl/ P 1 tbl/ P1b: Purl through the back loop
Short combinations of stitches	MB: Make bobble SSK: Slip, Slip, Knit SKP: Slip, knit and pass the slipped stitch over the knitted

	stitch
Repetition of stitches	When stitching, you will need to repeat as many stitches as you can and the number of stitches that you need to repeat are enclosed in asterisks. Take a look at the example below: *k2,p2*: repeatedly Knead two stitches together, purl stitches as long as possible.
Position of yarn	This is used in creating slipped stitches. WYIB: with yarn in back WYIF: with yarn in front
Beginnings and endings	This refers on how you need to start or end your knit stitch. BO: bind off CO: cast on
Overall pattern	This refers to the type of stitch pattern that you need to make for your knitted fabric. st st: stockinette stitch rev St st: reverse stockinette g st: garter stitch
Cable instructions	LT: left twist RT: right twist FC: front cross LC: left cross

	BC: back cross RC: right cross
Color changes	MC: Main color CC: Contrasting color
Decreases	This creates the tapered look as the stitches are decreased. K2tog: two stitches needed to be knitted together as one thereby decreasing the row.
Increases	This allows you to increase the number of stitches thus increasing the row. M1: Make one stitch KFB: Knit purl PFB: Purl into the front and back of a stitch
Positional abbreviations	REM: remaining FOLL: following BEG: beginning CONT: continue INCL: including

Chapter 4 Essential Materials for Knitting

Every extraordinary artisan requires a particular apparatus arrangement to execute his skill or trade appropriately. Paintbrushes and canvases are required by painters, mud and various metal tools are required by artists, and wire and dabs are needed by makers of gems!

With regards to knitting, it tends to be hard to tell what you do and don't require when you're first beginning. Without a doubt, you realize you need a skein of yarn and needles, yet what sort of yarn and what kind of needles? What different sorts of knitting materials would it be a good idea for one to obtain other than the self-evident? What's more, what's so much discussion about thoughts?

Underneath, we've laid out all the starting knitting supplies you need in one suitable spot. This extreme knitting instruments rundown will give an exhaustive review of the essential supplies you ought to have available to make your knitting venture as fruitful and pleasant as could be allowed. Additionally, these instruments can make knitting significantly simpler, and that is constantly a success in our book!

Beginning another side interest is an energizing encounter! As a beginner knitter, you might be enticed to bounce in the vehicle, head directly to the closest art supply store, and purchase everything knitting-related you can get your hands on. Yet, hang on a second... it doesn't bode well to go on a fiber-filled shopping binge immediately. Instead, give yourself some an opportunity to learn about your knitting needs and needs before you begin making a lot of buys.

Take a couple of moments to look at our optimal knitting starter unit, and you'll be furnished with the information you need before confronting the apparently unlimited paths of starting knitting supplies.

Huge, Straight Knitting Needles

The key thing on our list of knitting apparatuses is a few big, straight knitting needles. It's best to start tremendously at the stage where you are starting first. Greater needles and thicker lightweight yarns are much simpler to deal with and are likely to save you a lot of long haul frustration.

US Size 13/9 mm straight kneading needles is a successful choice. These needles won't harm your hands the way littler sizes can do when you're just starting. You can discover that round needle rehearsals work best for you. When using roundabout needles – you may stitch customary items on them – you do not need to weave in the round, and the shorter size makes them easier to handle, so it may be beneficial to put resources into a few fliers as well.

Two extra sizes utilized regularly are US 8/5mm and US 10/6mm. We prescribed first purchasing these three sizes and afterward gathering different sizes varying.

There is a wide range of kinds of needles, yet in case you're searching for a financial limit amicable choice for your knitting starter pack, we prescribed aluminum or plastic. Be that as it may, remember these materials can be very elusive, and your knitting lines can undoubtedly sneak off your needles. As indicated by the specialists at marthastewart.com, bamboo or wood needles can be extraordinary decisions for novices since they're agreeable, and your join won't slide off as without any problem.

As the book states, "Needles are made of various materials, including metal, wood, bamboo, and plastic. The material you pick involves inclination; however, amateurs may like working with wood or bamboo needles since they are somewhat adaptable, are agreeable to utilize, and lines don't sneak off them as effectively as they do from metal or plastic needles."

"I think tenderfoots do the best starting with a medium-weight yarn (worsted is acceptable) and medium-sized straight needles, maybe somewhere close to US 7 and US 9. Something too small is hard to interpret what you're doing, and something too large can be difficult to manage. It's up to you what needle material you want, I'm a bamboo sweetheart, but you might have to try more than just that.

Embroidered artwork Needles (otherwise known as Yarn Needles)

Embroidered artwork needles will be needles with an eye sufficiently huge to string yarn through. These needles are normally plastic (however, in some cases metal) and very cheap. Yarn needles perform twofold responsibility since they can be utilized to weave in closes or to join creases together, which is decent for specific tasks like sweaters.

Remember, these needles are anything but difficult to lose, so we prescribe purchasing a little compartment to store them when not being used.

A Crochet Hook

It might appear to be illogical to recommend purchasing sew snares for a knitting starter pack, however, listen to us. Sew snares can spare your knitting on numerous events. The two greatest favorable circumstances of knit snares are their capacity to fix dropped fastens and to weave in closes. Without a doubt, you can do both of these things in different manners, however, for apprentice knitters, utilizing a stitch snare can be the least demanding and most direct strategy.

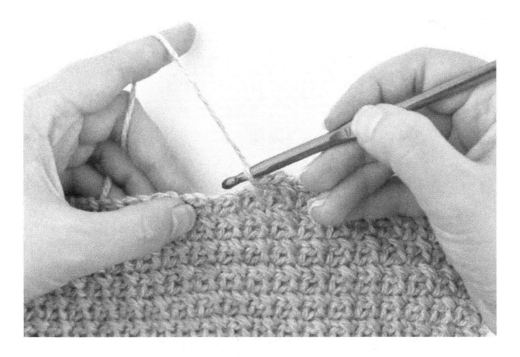

Consider purchasing a whole set since various yarns will require distinctive snare sizes. In addition, in the event that you choose, you need to take up a stitch, you'll as of now have a head start! Be that as it may, in case you're attempting to set aside cash or attempting to get a handle on what you really do or needn't bother with, a 3-4mm needle works extraordinary for most things.

Fasten Markers

Fasten markers are a brisk and simple approach to guarantee you effectively complete your knitting ventures. When you weave the join of your example, place the marker over the line you need to recall, and afterward keep knitting. The marker is just slipped to and fro between needles while you sew.

Join markers are incredibly modest and exceptionally helpful. You can put them on a join holder to abstain from losing them.

In this way, in case you're knitting a scarf that has a particular outskirt plan, you can utilize a line marker to make sure to sew the fringe once you go to that point in the example. This kind of fundamental knitting supply can spare you a great deal of exacerbation over the long haul.

Sew Counters

Numerous knitters – the two amateurs and fledglings – sing the gestures of recognition of them sew counters. We propose purchasing two – one to check fastens (as a rule when you're expanding or diminishing) and the other to tally lines.

As you would definitely know, there are some knitting designs were monitoring your lines is extra significant. A few counters slip directly on your needles, so you don't have to rifle around to change the number. You can likewise purchase a counter intended to stick around your neck.

Point Protectors

With regards to basic knitting apparatuses, point defenders perform two significant capacities. As the name recommends, point defenders should be utilized to shield the purposes of your needles from turning out to be harmed when not being used. Be that as it may, these little folks can likewise be utilized for shielding your lines from tumbling off the needles when you're not working them.

On the off chance that you choose to get up and quit knitting, you can put a point defender on the finish of the needle that holds the lines. In case you're taking a shot at an example that takes in excess of a few hours, it's fundamental to have the option to leave without the dread of losing your work. You can necessarily check where you left off with you sew counter and return to it when you're prepared.

As it were, you can breathe a sigh of relief, realizing your feline won't thump over the needle and take your yarn while you're away!

Estimating Tape

The kind of estimating tape you use will rely upon individual inclination. A few knitters choose the benevolent needle workers to use, and others utilize ones normally found in a knitting materials unit. An estimating tape is especially significant in case you're knitting a scarf since you should gauge your work to decide when it has gotten long enough to tie off.

An estimating tape can likewise be utilized to check your measurements. In any case, remember there are additionally extraordinary instruments called measures which can prove to be useful if the numbers on your needles ever focus on because you can check your needle size utilizing a measure.

Weave Counters

Numerous knitters – the two learners and apprentices – sing the commendations of their weave counters. We recommend purchasing two – one to tally join (for the most part when you're expanding or diminishing) and the other to tally columns.

As you would definitely know, there are some knitting designs were monitoring your lines is extra significant.

Chapter 5 What Are The Different Kinds of Yarns and Needles?

When you're remaining in the store before a masterminded rainbow of yarn, how would you choose which one is ideal for your next knitting venture? Here's all that you have to know past skim-perusing the name.

We should begin with the nuts and bolts: What is yarn? Yarn is a material generally made of either creature-based strands (sheep's fleece, mohair, angora), plant-based filaments (cotton, hemp, silk), or manufactured strands (polyester, nylon, rayon). These interlocked filaments (alluded to as utilizes) are spun together into thicker strands. The quantity of handles (for instance, a solitary employ yarn or two-utilize yarn) will influence the wrap, join definition, and general feel of the yarn. The employ tally factors into the accompanying classes:

Yarn Weight Categories

Classification 0: LACE

(Surmised EQUIVALENT OF 1 PLY)

This is the lightest load of yarn utilized for making doilies and other exquisite trim plans. Consequently, treat it tenderly to abstain from tangling or breakage.

Classes 1, 2, AND 3: SUPER FINE, FINE, AND LIGHT

(Inexact EQUIVALENT OF 2 TO 5 PLY)

This is appropriate for little things like socks, gloves, caps, or pieces of clothing for infants and kids. Cast on and off freely. In particular, fine yarn is normally alluded to as "sport weight."

Class 4: MEDIUM

(Inexact EQUIVALENT OF 8 TO 10 PLY)

Otherwise called "worsted," this is a famous load among knitters of all aptitude levels since it gives incredible line definition in sweaters, scarves, caps, and gloves. Thick join weaved in conventional Aran yarn of this weight can improve the glow of fiber.

Classifications 5 AND 6: BULKY AND SUPER BULKY

(Estimated EQUIVALENT OF 12 TO 14 PLY)

Materials of this weight produce quick tasks on huge needles. Think: stout scarves, tosses, and covers. This kind of yarn is useful for amateurs since it produces extends rapidly and is additionally useful for cutting edge knitters who are hoping to make something extraordinary with novel yarn. Weave free, huge join for ideal space. Unevenly spun yarn like boucle, chenille, or slubby yarn will create lopsided sews and a diminished join definition.

REGULAR FIBERS

FLEECE

Spun from the downy of sheep and one of the most famous yarns, fleece is accessibly evaluated and simple to deal with. It functions admirably for knitwear pieces of clothing in both the winter for its sturdiness and protection from dampness just as the late spring for its breathability and dampness wicking. It's regularly blended in a mix with different filaments to improved sturdiness. Normally, fleece is a rich white and consequently can be colored a scope of hues. Tragically, fleece is inclined to pilling after some time.

Care: Gently hand wash in lukewarm water.

MOHAIR

This cushy, sumptuous fiber is known for its delicate sheen and gentility regardless of being one of the hottest creature filaments. It is costlier than fleece. Mohair is extremely flexible extending and springing back to shape so it opposes wrinkling and drooping. Since it is so cushy, it tends to be difficult to weave particularly in the event that you need characterized fastens. It is frequently mixed with silk or fleece to include weight.

YARN NEEDLES

They are a bigger version of regular sewing needles. It is mainly used for weaving at the end of the project. Like hooks, they have different sizes according to yarn's weight. They are mostly made of plastic, but other materials are available. There are a few differences between this and sewing needles:

They are a bit longer than regular sewing needles.

The yarn needles are dull and less sharp than sewing needles.

Mechanism of action is just like sewing needles, so if you know how to sew, then you can work with them as well. They can be replaced by tapestry needles, which look very similar to them.

How to use them?

There are many ways you can use them

- At the end of the work, you will find that there are many ends of yarn left hanging on the side of your project. To get rid of them and secure your work, you need to weave them into place. This is done by using yarn needles.
- Granny square is a popular pattern design for crochet. Most of the time, you have to stitch them together by a mattress stitch or whip stitch. This is done by a yarn needle.
- It is used when joining dolls together or making other embellishments.
- When making surface stitches and decoration, you need this as well.
- Sometimes you get holes in your work, and you need to fix them. For repair, yarn needles play a major role.

Chapter 6 Step-By-Step For Beginners

The Essential Stitches For Knitting

The Knit Stitch (K)

1. Together with the yarn behind the work, however, the right-hand needle from the left through the entire front of the first stitch around the left-hand needle.

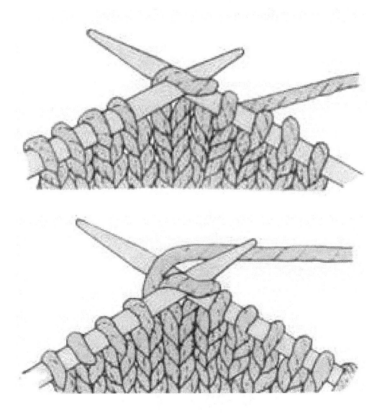

2. Wind the yarn over the right-hand man needle.

3. Pull Through A Loophole.

4. Slip the initial stitch from the left-hand needle. Do it again until all of the stitches have already been in movement through the entrusted for the right-hand needle.

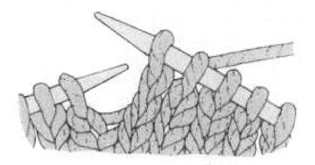

To Knit Right Into The Rear Of A Stitch (KB1).

This technique is also used, along with other textured stitch patterns, to create a twisted effect on the rib. Insert the needle on the left-hand side into the rear of the thread, then stick to steps 2 to 4 for the knit thread.

The Purl Stitch (P)

1. Along with the yarn at the front end of the work, position the right-hand needle from the left through leading of the initial stitch over the left-hand needle.

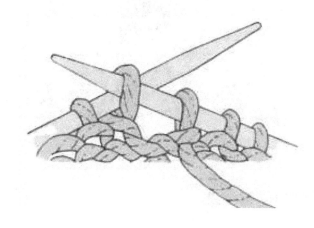

2. Wind the yarn around the right-hand needle.

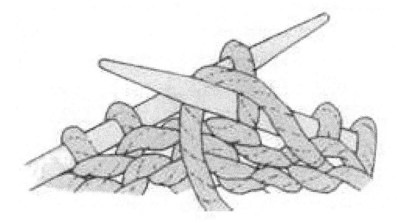

3. Draw a loop with the back.

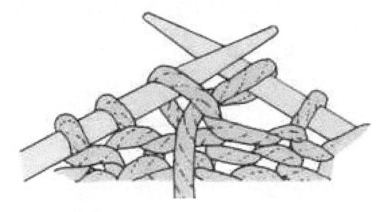

4. Slip the initial stitch off the left-hand needle.

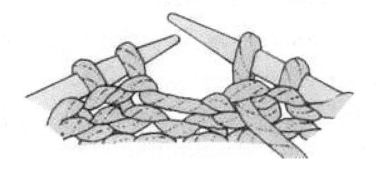

To Purl Into the Rear of a Stitch (PB1)

Position the needle directly into the back of this stitch over the left-hand needle from right behind and also carry the factor on the right-hand needle to the front, then adhere to steps 2 to 4 for that purl stitch.

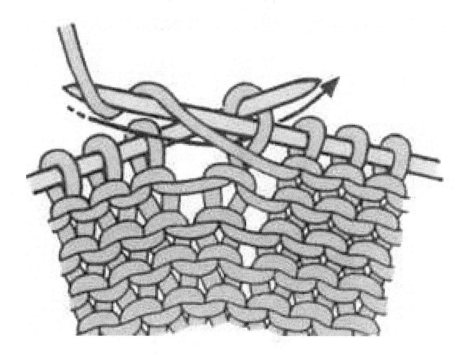

The Garter Stitch

The garter stitch is usually made by making every row to be a knit row, the original row generally getting the ideal part.

The same effect can likewise be arrived at by working every row as purl.

Equipping Stitch

Stocking stitch comprises one row of knit stitches honored by one row of purl stitches, and you start with a knit row that is the right facet of the work.

Reverse Stitch.

Reverse equipping stitch comprises one row of purl stitches adhered to by one row of knit stitches, beginning with a purl row, which is the appropriate side of the job.

Ribbing

Ribbing is an elastic textile that is typically used for garment edgings. Both most normal kinds are 1x1 rib, which is developed by rotating one knit stitch and also one purl stitch and even 2x2 rib, which is formed by alternating two knit stitches and also two purl stitches. Care should be taken to purl the stitches which were weaved on the previous row and also vice versa.

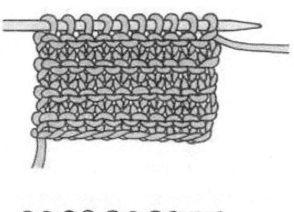

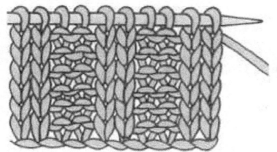

Knit One Below (K1B).

This stitch is in use in Fishermen's rib. Put the right-hand needle right into the next stitch, yet in the row listed below the stitch on the left-hand needle. Knit the stitch as usual.

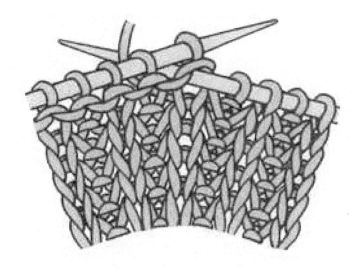

How to Knit in the Round.

If you would certainly love to knit sleeves or socks, weaving in the round is an excellent ability to have. Determine if you wish to knit on round needles so you can quickly knit tubular shapes. If you like, you can make use of several dual pointed needles to knit in the round as well as form your material. Utilizing a magic loop technique is another prominent method to interweave in the circles using round needles considering that it's a fast way to knit several rows

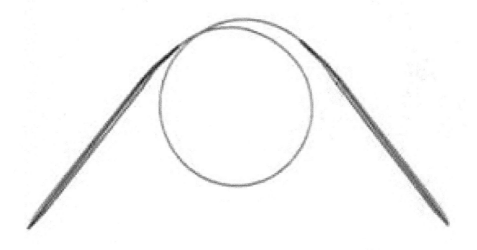

Cast your stitches onto a round needle. Select any round cord that you're comfortable with making use of as long as it's suitable for your task. Utilize a circular needle with a wire that's shorter than the diameter of what you're weaving. If you are knitting a jacket using a 34-inch (86-cm) diameter, start using a needle having a wire that's not more than 29 inches (76-cm) long. The team on as many stitches as you need for the knitting job.

You can get cables from 9 to 60-inches (22 centimeters to 1.5-meters) long.

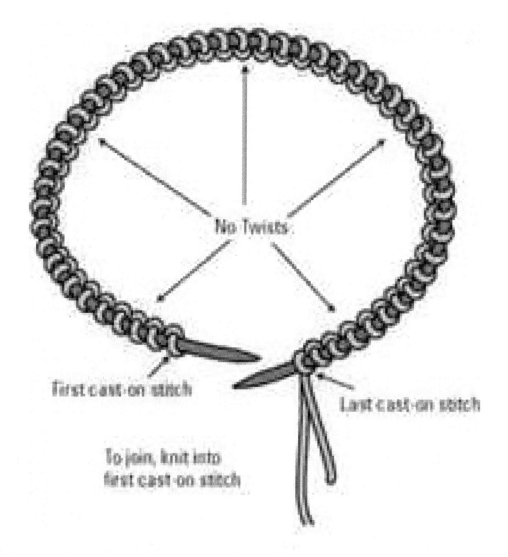

Glide the stitches onto the wire and needle along with the functioning yarn once you have cast on as many stitches as you need to maneuver the stitches down onto the cable connection. The sutures will be near the notion of the remaining needle.

Look for twisted stitches. Smooth the stitches, so they're facing similarly as well as aren't turned. The cast-on stitches shouldn't loophole or spin over the cord. It's vital to do this before you start weaving, or the fabric will undoubtedly have a warped shape that you can't undo later.

Place a stitch marker on your needle. As you prepare to start knitting, place a stitched pen on the very best pointer. The stitch pen will undoubtedly help you in monitoring the number of rows you've made.

You may get logical stitch markers at the craft shops, sewing retailers, and also some food markets.

Knit the first row. Place the right needle pointer into the stitch on the left needle. Cover the working yarn around the needle and also move the finished knit stitch onto the appropriate needle. Keep knitting up until you've knitted the whole row and also are back at the stitch marker.

 Ensure that you're knitting with the functioning yarn and not the yarn tail.

Continue steadily to knit until you've arrived at the desired span. Maintain knitting every row until your textile options are as long as your pattern advises. Be aware that every time you attain the stitch pen, you've finished yet another row.

If you're working from a pattern, keep in mind that you're always working with the best side of the material.

Weaving with Double Pointed Needles

Throw your stitches onto hands down the double-pointed needles. Abide by your structure and toss on as many stitches as needed. Check out the design to see how many double sharp needles you'll need to knit in the round.

Split the stitches between the various other double pointed needles. Equally split the variety of stitches onto the array of needles your pattern require. For instance, if you cast on 15 stitches and also the model requires you to utilize three dual sharp needles, slide five stitches onto each needle.

Keep in mind that you'll require an additional double-pointed needle that you'll utilize to interweave.

If you can't separate the stitches uniformly, the style should define how exactly to show the stitches between all the double-pointed fine needles.

You are building the needles right into a triangular. Transfer the fine needles, so they're all coming in contact with each other and also fastened in a triangle kind.

Glide the stitches to the biggest mark of the cable and, also, divide them. Work with your fingertips to slip the stitches right down to the biggest mark of the versatile cable connection.

Hold the fine needles, so the operating yarn is all set for knitting. Relocate the hands holding the circular needle.

Glide the stitches from the trunk needle onto the wire. Pull the trunk needle out; therefore, the yarn slides onto the line.

Ensure that the stitches do not get turned once you transfer those to the trunk needle. The row of stitches that you cast on find yourself being underneath the edge of one's knitting job.

You can find tubular knitting in the circular needle when you've finished 2-3 rows of stitches.

It is used during shaping, on make joints, for example, and forms typically the final row of the task. Always throw off in the design, my spouse and, i.e., when servicing stocking stitch empty knit wise on the knit row and also purl wise on the purl row and even when departing ribbing, achieve this just like you were remaining for the rib. Most style stitches could be complied with when casting off.

Casting Off Knit-Wise

Knit the first two stitches. * Using the left-hand needle, lift the very first stitch over the second as well as drop it off the needle. Knit the next stitch as well as repeat from the photo shown below:

Purl the first two stitches. * Using the left-hand needle, lift the initial stitch over the second and also drop it off the needle. Purl the next stitch and also repeat from below image.

Casting Off With A Crochet Hook

It saves significant amounts of time if you start using a crochet hook to throw off. Take care of the crochet hook as though it had been the right-hand needle, and besides, knit or purl the initial two stitches in the most common method. * Take the next stitch via the original, knit or purl the next stitch in addition to repeat it.

This approach is especially useful whenever a loosened, a versatile abandoned edge is necessary, as it is possible to gently release the stitch nonetheless within the crochet hook to make sure that the elasticity is indeed maintained.

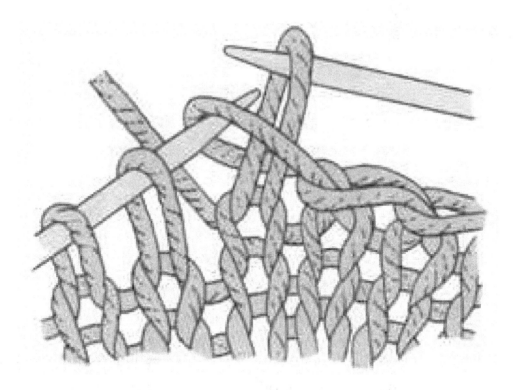

Tension is Very Important

We have worried about the value of weaving a stress example before starting work.

Chapter 7 Techniques of Knitting

Technique How to Knit: Casting On

"Throwing on" is the name for the system used to get the principal column of join on the needle, fundamental in beginning knitting. There are a few techniques for throwing on, however the one that we will learn here is known as the "long-tail cast-on." It's a flexible and solid cast-on that you can use for most undertakings.

Technique How to Knit: The Long-Tail Cast-On

Figure out how to weave the long-tail cast on in knitting with this selective how to sew for tenderfoot's asset.

Leaving a long tail (around 2 1/2" to 3" for each line to be thrown on), make a slipknot and spot on right needle.

Spot thumb and pointer of left hand between yarn closes with the goal that working yarn is around forefinger and the last part is around the thumb.

Secure the finishes with your separate fingers just a few crawls under the needles. Keep the palm upwards, and make a V of thread.

Bring the needle up through the circle on the thumb, snatch the principal strand around pointer with the needle, and return down through circle on the thumb.

Drop circle off the thumb and, putting thumb back in V setup, tenderly fix coming about join on the needle.

Be certain not to cast-on too firmly or freely — join ought to effectively slide to and for on the needle without looking free and "loopy."

Fledgling Knitting Practice: Cast on 20 lines. Presently remove the entirety of the join from the needle (I know, I know...) and cast on 20 lines once more. Rehash this procedure until you feel extremely great with this cast-on. At the point when you are simply figuring out how to sew, it requires a significant stretch of time to get that muscle memory instilled, so keep at it! It'll come, I guarantee.

In the event that you are searching for help on the best way to begin knitting, this workshop is for you. With exercises intended for starting knitting needs, you'll get more than two hours of guidance covering lines, basic errors, and in any event, knitting in the round, yarn types and completing methods. Look no farther than this how to weave video to kick you off! Download the Getting Started Knitting video today.

Technique How to Knit: Making a Slipknot

This cast-on begins with a slip hitch, which is a bunch that takes care of effectively once you place it on the needle.

Figure out how to make a slipknot the correct method to begin throwing on for your knitting right now to weave for apprentice's asset.

With the last part of the yarn in your palm, fold the working yarn over your file and center fingers and lay the working yarn over the last part, framing a X.

Stretch your fingers a bit, and move the working yarn from the back of your hand through your fingertips.

Pull this circle up somewhat while holding the last part of the yarn to frame a bunch.

Spot the circle onto the knitting needle and pull working yarn to change the strain.

Apprentice Knitting Practice: Make a lot of slip hitches, again and again and over!

Furthermore, for every stage of knitting, there are important factors to be considered. Slip knot is the first step for casting on. Here, pull out about 30 inches, which is about 76cm out of the ball of yarn. The slip knot is made at a point of 24 inches, which is 61cm. The tail part is on the left, while the working yarn on the right.

1.   Make a clockwise ring with the working yarn at the top and the tail at the bottom. With the thumb and forefinger of your left hand, tweak the loop and use your right hand to drape the working yarn behind the loop.

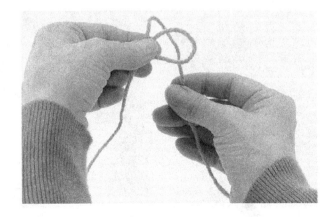

2.   Hold the needle with your right hand, go below the thread of working yarn, which is arranged across the back of the loop.

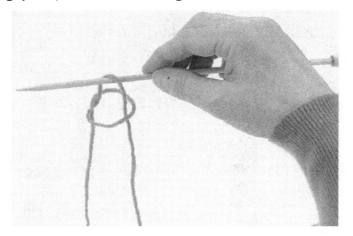

3.   The next thing is to drop the loop on your left hand. Pull the working yarn and the tail to help ease the tension and snug the coil on the needle. After that, the slip knot forms the loop on the needle. The slip knot makes the first stitch on the needle when casting on is made.

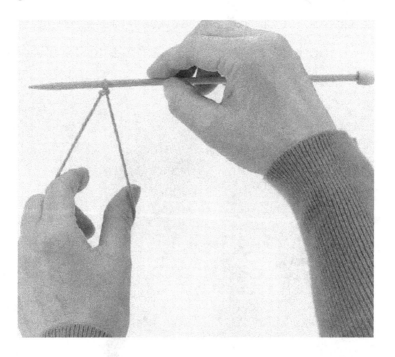

CAST ON (CO)

The long tail cast on is the most prevalent technique used while casting on. The name cast on is derived from the fact that half of the cast on stitch is formed using a tail of yarn. And so, before you commence, ensure that your tail is long enough to cast-on your desired number of stitches.

To be on a safe side, allow about an inch(2.5cm) for every stitch to be cast on. Also, you can wrap the yarn around the needle used for each stitch, add 8 inches, which are 20cm to get a good measure.

Take note of the following steps:

1. On the right needle, begin with the slip knot. Ensure that the tail is about 24 inches, which is 61cm long; this will allow for casting on about 20 stitches. Let the working yarn be on the right while the tail on the left. From behind, place the forefinger and thumb of your left hand between the working yarn and tail. Be careful to let the tail be draped over your thumb while the working yarn placed over your forefinger.

2. The other fingers on your left hand should be used to hold both strands tightly against your palm firmly. Spread your forefinger and your thumb apart with the palm of your left hand, which is facing you. You'll notice that the yarn will form a diamond

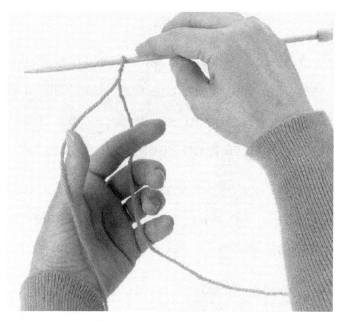

3. With your right hand, pull the top of the diamond. whereby it appears like a slingshot

4. Through the loop on the thumb, Insert the needle through an upward position

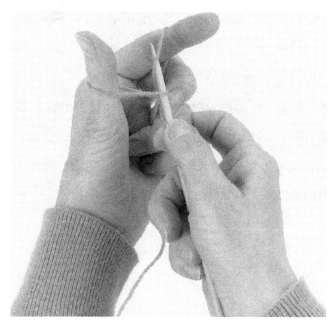

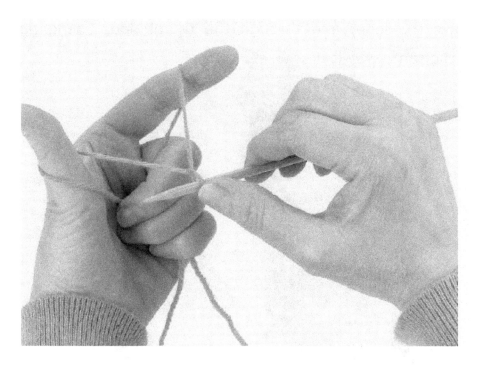

5. To pick a loop, fix the needle to your right hand and then go over the top, after which go under the working yarn fix on your forefinger.

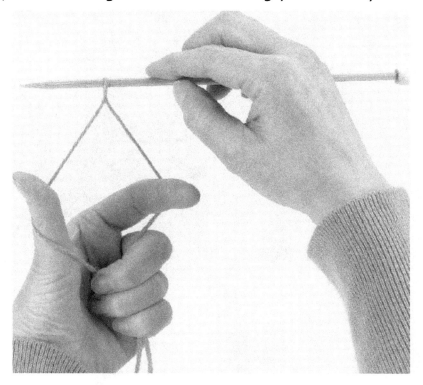

6. Pull down the loop, and through the thumb loop, send back the needle the same way it first went.

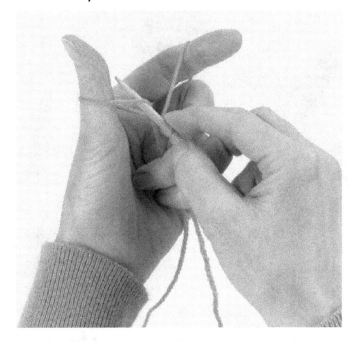

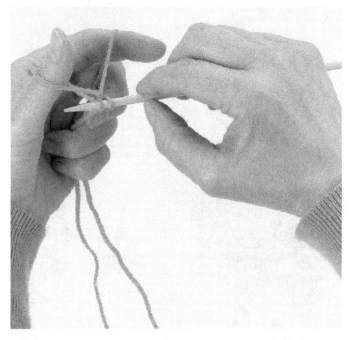

7. In the stage, out of the original loop, drop your thumb and then fix it again on the tail side to form a diamond, as you saw in step 2. You'll see that a new stitch will be formed on the needle, but this is loosed. Next, spread apart the forefinger and thumb of your left hand; this will pull both strands at the base of the new stitch till it is not firmly (not tight) on the needle.

8. At this point, the 2nd cast-on stitch is completed. In the slingshot position, reposition the yarn and repeat step four to seven until these motions are properly memorized.

PRACTICE SWATCH

Knit (K, k)

The aim of swatching is to put together the fabric of your finished garment as much as possible. Therefore, it's imperative to knit your swatch using the same condition for knitting your projects; with the same size and material of needles.

Once you have learned and mastered the art of casting on, the next thing to do is make a practice swatch with the aid of a medium weight yarn (worsted weight yarn) which is weightier than double knitting yarn, crochet thread or baby weight yarn. This is done by using a single point needle of size 8 (5 mm) 9 inches (23 cm). Cast on 20 stitches and follow the steps below to achieve your desired result.

1. Take hold of the needle with the cast-on stitches on your left hand while the needle tip is pointed to the right. As you work on each row of the stitches, the stitches will be shifted from the left needle to the right one. Eventually, the rows become complete when all the stitches have been moved from the left needle to the right needle.

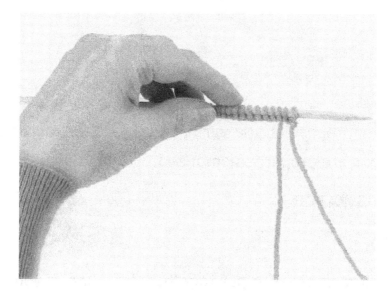

2. Next, hold the empty needle in your right hand, as the tip points to the left. On both needles the thumb and middle finger should

hold the needle gently. Attach the right needle to the first stitch on the left needle, which is the one closest to the tip as you pass through the loop above the bump, as you work from front to rear. At this time, both needles will be at the back of the strand with which you are working.

3.   The fingers of the left hand should be used to grip the needles so that it forms an 'X' sign. This time, the right needle will be at the back.

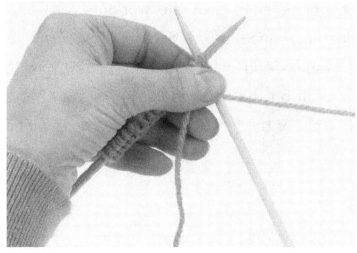

4. With your right hand, pick up the ball of yarn you are working with and in an anticlockwise direction, let it wrap around the needle on the right hand. At this point, the yarn will be between the two needles. As time go by, you'll be acquainted with learning unique ways of grasping the working yarn. But for now, I'll advise that you hold the working yarn in between your thumb and forefinger of your right hand.

5. With a bit of tension, hold the working yarn and needle on the right together, slope down the needle to the left and bring it towards you, as you draw the yarn you're working with through the first stitch on the left needle. You'll see that the right needle will be in front of the left needle, having a new loop of yarn on it.

6.   To the right, slide the right needle and then off the end of the needle on the left, as you take off the newly formed stitch from the left needle. When this is done, the original stitch will come out with it. At this point, a knit stitch is being completed.

7. The next step is to replicate what you've done in steps two to six across the remaining stitches on the left needle. You'll notice that the needle on the right becomes the "full" needle. Here, one knitted row has been formed.

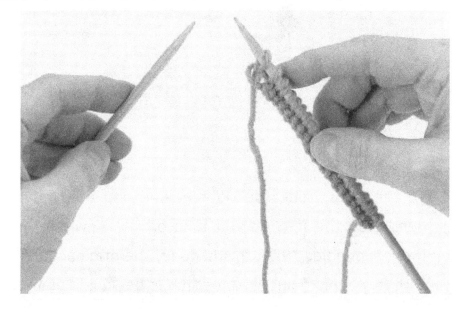

8. To begin a new row, take the needle on your right hand to the left with the tip being pointed to the right.

    But before then, lightly tug the bumps at the bottom of the new stitches, and ensure that the yarn you're knitting with comes out of the bottom of the bump which is on the stitch closest to the tip of the needle on the left. Make a repetition of the steps in two to six across the row.

9.   As you perform your practice switch, continue to work on new rows until you're comfortable in making knit stitches.

The technique you have just learned whereby your right-hand wraps round the yarn around the needle is termed "The English method." For the continental method of knitting, it is the left hand that wraps the yarn, which is around the needle.

.

Chapter 8 Knitting Patterns for Beginners

Knitting Patterns

As a beginner knitter, you may find it challenging reading knitting patterns. What you will likely see is a coded writeup, filled with abbreviations. But I need to tell you that reading a knitting pattern is not exactly difficult.

We will discuss how to read and understand knitting patterns in this part. But first, let's consider the typical set of information that is encoded into a knitting pattern.

Necessary Pieces of Information on a Knitting Pattern

- Skill Level: More often than not, this is the first information that is included in a knitting pattern after the name and picture of the knitted material. This is great for beginner knitters, because you can know the materials that you should attempt and those you shouldn't try to knit. For instance, when you see 'intermediate' or 'advanced' on a pattern, you simply skip it till you have become an intermediate or advanced knitter, respectively.

- Size: The size of the project is only essential if you are making a material that needs to fit on the user. However, for a start, you will be working with projects that don't need to fit precisely on the wearer. Such projects include scarves, blankets, among others. As you become a more professional knitter, you should check the size of the fabric before knitting.

- Gauge: Like size, the gauge is not essential for projects that don't require fitting on the user.
- Yarn and needle sizes: This part will tell you the size and type of yarn and knitting needles that were used in the project, as well as any other special tools that you will need during the project. You don't need to use the exact type of yarn that was used in the project. You can use yarn of similar weight or thickness.
- Abbreviations: More often than not, abbreviations are used to denote instructions in knitting patterns.

Directions for different stitches:

Ribbing

Ribbing is utilized to hold the sleeves of sleeves, edges of necks, caps, and bottoms of sweaters fit as a fiddle. To make a ribbing effectively you will require: for K1 P1 (sew 1, purl 1) ribbing a various of two, or for K2 P2 (sew 2, purl 2) ribbing a numerous of four. You can utilize your check swatch as a proving ground for various stitches; for example, attempt 4 crawls of K 1 P 1, and afterward 4 creeps of K2 P2. The weave stitches will look smooth on the two sides and will pull the example in as though it had flexible in it. The following is an example of K1, P1 ribbing. The subsequent photograph is K2, P2 ribbing.

1) K1, P1 ribbing.

2)   K2, P2 ribbing has been added to the top, notice how it pulls the texture more tightly.

Seed stitch

You need an odd number of stitches for seed stitch. A seed stitch is rotating K1, P1 each line with the goal that the stitches are balanced from each other. To make things simple, you would start each line with a K1 and proceed *P1, K1*, rehash between *'s, as far as possible of the column. Proceed on like this for four inches with the goal that you have a little example of a seed stitch. As you come you will weave where there are a purl and purling where there is a sew on the last column. The stitches are balanced, if they end up in a state of harmony with one another, you will have a rib.

Greenery stitch

Underneath I have given directions to making the greenery stitch in a run of the mill knitting guidelines design. In the passage that adheres to the directions, I have explained a piece on the off chance that that may assist you with seeing better what you are doing.

Line 1: K2, P2 across Row 2: K2, P2 across Row 3: P2, K2 across Row 4: P2, K2 over

For this example, rehash lines 1-4 for 4 inches. For the greenery stitch, you need a significant number of stitches in a numerous of four.

Row1: You will K2, P2 over. You end with P2, so you will have the option to start

Row2: with K2 and go across as you did in Row 1.

Column 3: The third line starts the contrary example, which means P2, K2 over. Recall that when you start you can slip the primary stitch as though to purl and purl the subsequent stitch, at that point K2. You will do the P2, K2 across and should end with a K2 (Row3).

Row4: Slip the primary stitch as though to purl, at that point P1, *K2, P2* across (Remember that when you see two marks in knitting directions, it implies you should rehash the guidelines between them). After these four columns, start again with the K2, P2, which is a rehash of Row1. You can see that each example is four lines. Doing Row 1 twice and Row 3 twice makes the four-column design arrangement.

Sampler Scarf

Make a sampler scarf which has fastener stitch pushes on both start and end, and 2 to 4 stitches of a weave on either edge to make an outskirt of tie stitch. Attempt stockinet stitch with minor departure from seed stitch to make structures all through. On the off chance that you put a ribbing stitch in the center where the rear of the neck will be, it will be smaller than the remainder of the scarf. Authoritative off or pushing off to complete your scarf. The following are a few investigations utilizing weave and purl for plans.

1)   Purl the first and keep going stitches on the principal push. On the second column P the primary stitch, K the subsequent stitch, P until the second to last stitch (K) in the example since you are on 'an inappropriate' side. On the 'right' side you will K3 then P1, K until four stitches stay, at

that point P1, K3. Simply keep moving you sew or purl in toward the inside on each column until they compromise. At that point, you begin going out with the plan until you get to the edge.

2)   This is similar to an Argyle plan without the hues. You can utilize diagram paper to make your structures. On the off chance that you know your measurements, you will have the option to tell precisely what it will resemble. If your lines and stitches are not square it will likely be somewhat twisted; more precious stone than square.

3)   This is an examination where I made a precious stone with purl stitches.

4)   The example above is done two by two, moving more than one stitch each time. The accompanying directions accept a 20-stitch wide example with 2 sew stitches on each side to forestall twisting along the edges. There are 16 stitches in the example. 'K' is a weave, 'P' is purl.

Start on a sew push, odd lines will be the correct side, even lines will be posterior.

Line 1: K9, P2, K9.

Column 2: K2, P6, K4, P6, K2.

Line 3: K7, P2, K2, P2, K7.

Row 4: K2, P4, K2, P4, K2, P4, K2.

Line 5: K5, P2, K2, P2, K2, P2, K5.

Line 6: K2, P2, K2, P2 K4, P2, K2, P2, K2. Line 7: K3, P2, K2, P2, K2, P2, K2, P2, K3.

Line 7-8: K4, P2, K2, P4, K2, P2, K4.

Line 9: K2, P1, K2, P2, K2, P2, K2, P2, K2, P1, K2.

Lines 10-13: Follow Rows 6-9. Rehash this the same number of times as you like.

The clear squares are purled on the 'right' half of the undertaking. On 'an inappropriate' side you will weave the clear squares as opposed to purling them. Charts are regularly perused from the option to the left and the base up since you are knitting from the base up. Else you will have a topsy turvy structure. The concealed territory on the correct side is sewed, the clear is purled. On an inappropriate side, you will purl the concealed territory and knitting where the clear is.

If you are purling on push 2, you will begin the left half of line 2, and continue up the draft in a crisscross way. Notice that I obscured lines 6-9 a subsequent time so you can perceive how it rehashes. The highest point of the chart doesn't exactly go similar to the knitting in the photograph. At the point when you get to the highest point of the chart and you need to proceed, return down to push 6 and rehash the columns 6 through 9 the same number of times as you like. With only a pencil and some chart paper, you can test diagramming your geometric plans. Make sure to peruse them from the option to left and start at the baseline and continue upwards. At the point when you are on an inappropriate side/purl side, you will follow the example from the left to one side. Your knitting goes to and for, as a crisscross, that is how you'll follow the diagram. Indeed, when you backpedal on the even lines, on the purl side, you will purl the dull squares and sew the clear squares.

If you are knitting in the round, which I put in a later exercise, you will begin at the base right and proceed up the diagram moving from the correct side to one side. Now you are knitting to and for, so you will sew from the privilege to one side on odd columns, from the left to one side on even lines, in a crisscross design.

Knitted Beanie

Size: Adult sized.

Yarn: 100 yards of medium worsted weight, size 4.

Needles: Size 8.

Tools Required: Yarn, needle.

Gauge Instructions: 16 stitches = 4 inches.

Pattern:

- Cast on 74 stitches
- For the first 6 rows create a rib stitch across – knit 1, purl 1

- Then knit one row and purl the next until the piece measures 7 inches, from the cast on edge. Be sure to purl the last row
- For the next row, knit 2 together (k2tog) across
- Purl the next row
- K2tog across for the next row
- Cut 12 inches of yarn and thread it onto the yarn needle
- Pull carefully from the needle the last row of knitting and thread the needle after each stitch, pull tightly and stitch the seam shut down.

Baby Blanket

Difficulty: Beginner – pattern is reversible.

Size: 30 inches wide, 33 inches long.

Yarn: 5 balls of chunky yarn – size 5.

Needles: A circular needle, size 10.

Tools Required: Stitch markers, a large eye blunt needle.

Gauge Instructions: 12 stitches and 20 rows = 4 inches

Pattern: NB – the circular needle is used to accommodate the large number of stitches so work back and forth as if working on straight needles.

Cast on 90 stitches

For the first 6 rows, knit the seed stitch:

- For the first row, knit one and purl one all the way across

- For the second row, purl the knit stitches and knit the purl stitches and repeat this 4 times

Row 7 – work the seed stitch over the first 5 stitches for the side border

Purl 16 stitches

Knit 16; purl 16 all the way across until the last 5 stitches

Work the seed stitch for the final 5 stitches

Row 8 – work in the seed stitch in the first and last 5 stitches, and knit across in between

Rows 9 to 160 – repeat rows 7 and 8

Row 161 to 166 – repeat instructions for the top 6 rows, making the seed stitch for the top border

Bind off and weave in the ends.

Chapter 9 Advanced Knitting Patterns

Fair Isle Bottle Cozy

Materials

- For background color, take 18 yards of color A. For pattern color, take color B of 10 yards. For both colors, take medium weight cotton or cotton mix yarn of mediumweight cotton or cotton mix yarn

- Take set of four size 7 US (4.5 mm) twofold pointed weaving needles

- Bottle Cozy Knitting Chart copy

- Scissors and yarn needle

Gauge

Use 22.5 stitches for each 4 inches (around 5.5 fasten per inch) in design. Gauge is not that basic, but rather a well huge gauge will make the pattern not fit the container.

Size

Take the size around 3.75 inches tall and very nearly 8 inches around. To fit a standard measured refreshment bottle.

Directions

- Make 42 stitches on pattern using color A (grey in the example pattern). Separate onto 3 needles, join in the round, being mindful so as not to contort fastens. Place a fasten marker if sought to check the start of the round (however it will be clear before long where the round finishes)

- Work the Bottle Cozy outline, recollecting to work from base to beat and from right to left on each round, changing colors as expected to work the design.

- Bind off in shading A. Cut wool and weave in finishes.

Giant Tweed Blanket

There is nothing better than getting cozy on a cold night in front of the TV or with a good book. This blanket uses tweed yarn which is better for everyday use and tends to last longer than some other yarns and fibers which mean you can get the most from this blanket! (Plus, it's cuddly too!)

You Will Need

- 15 Balls of Bulky Tweed Yarn

- Size 50 Needles

Note: you may not be able to fit all of the stitches on the needles so try purchasing circular or extension needles to hold all the stitches.

Pattern

Row 1: Cast on 50 stitches

Row 2: Using the knit stitch, knit in continual rows until you have around 7" of project so far. This is the first edging of your blanket.

Row 3: Knit and purl the fallowing rows. (K1 P1) until you have 50" of total project.

Row 4: Using the knit stitch, repeat row 2 so that you repeat the first edge on the opposite side.

Row 5: Cast off and weave together the ends.

Jacket sleeveless

Pins No. 9, and fingering or black Berlin.

Attach 98 stitches. Attach. Wear 12 circles. 12 circles.

13th row — knit 16, knit 30 wool over yarn, knit 6, cut wool, knit 30, knit 16.

The alternating lines are simple.

The fifteenth row — knit 17, knit 30 on yarn, knit 8, wool on, knit 30 on fur, knit 17.

17th row — 18 sweater, 30 knit fur, 10 knit, over, 30, knit, over, 18 knit wool.

Go for 60 rows in this direction.

On the other hand, remove 60 stitches on 33 rows back and forth.

Thirty-third row — 5 stitches tossed away (this must be at the beginning of the row); the remainder knit square.

Thirty-fourth row —the neck to 2 next to the cast stitches at the end of the row. Reduce and cast off for the shoulder for 31 sets. So, put 16 stitches under the belt, then take the 66 under the pants on the bottom. Do 16 lines basic, then decrease by 38 lines for shoulder at the end of each section. Jump here for the face.

Then take the other arm off 16. On the other hand, take the remaining 60 stitches and make 32 rows on the other leg. Cast off 5 for the neck and then each for 32 rows at the end of each alternate section.

Sew on the arms.

Take up 53 stitches on the right hand and perform 2 straight lines. Create the buttonhole per 12 stitches; then knit the wool 3 times round the needle on the next thread; knit the first component, knit the second, knit the third part of this pattern.

Build three more rows and cast off.

Perform the same number of rows and sew buttons on the other foot. This is better to place a little piece of tissue beneath the base because the buttons are perfect for taking off.

Take the stitches of the waist; every 4 stitches.

Second row — increase, Imitate to the middle, and again rise.

Repeat these six-row rises. Then growing in the middle 3 times. Do 4 more lines, and then 6 lines of the much coarser pin in brioche; do no increases now.

Cast down. Take back. Take the stitches around your arm, minimize by 5 times each alternating row for 4 rows, and create 4 rows with smaller sticks. Cast down. Take back.

This lightens the jacket to create violet or blue boundaries.

Crochet the ends on.

These are quite good, warm gifts for the needy, made of gross yarn. But, since the design is a tiny figure, there must be more stitching, particularly the tail.

Baby's Hat, Style Marguerite

This is achieved in two colors, white leg, and blue or rose hat. Triple coat of Shetland with four sticks. Number 15.

Project 48. Set 48. Knit 3, 3 round pearl. Bind 3 for the next 3, Pearl 3.

Seventh-round — Work either of third series striped patterns for two inches (or you can rib the first half of the leg and knit the rest straight); combine blue and work I single round. Bring 22 to the heel and knit, not loops.

Knit 3, paid 3, reversing every fourth side, to create tiny squares in line with the beginning. After 18 rows are done, take the 13th then the 14th, then change the heel in a pattern, taking care to reverse the positions in the proper order. Taking twelve stitches on one leg. Reduce the instep on each hand before you have 48 stitches; it evens the squares. If 1 square is done (counting 1 1 from the front leg), decrease any other round for the teeth on each side until just 30 are remaining. You have to be cautious to render decreases only opposite each other on the boot foot so that they are even and square.

Knit the wrong hand together. Crochet the scalloped edge of the same color as the boot on the leg and loop the rope around the foot. Cast on 50 with Andalusian wool and mark it with pink spots at frequent intervals until done.

Perform so with a needle in the thread. Crochet the boot with a top with the same color and apply a touch with rosette. Belt in hand. You will, of example, make pink ribbon holes across your ankle.

Another approach is to render 4 rows of knitting, then I row pearl, I row, I row, I row pearl. Then just see the straight row. The garments feel pretty sprinkled with filoselle rather than leather.

Fingerless Mittens

Difficulty: Beginner – pattern is reversible.

Size: 10 inches around and 18 inches long.

Yarn: 2 balls of worsted weight yarn.

Needles: Size 7.

Tools Required: Yarn, needle, stitch markers.

Gauge Instructions: 20 stitches and 28 rows = 4 inches.

Pattern:

Cast on 66 stitches

For the first row:

•   On the right side knit 2 stitches

Then purl 2 and knit 2 all the way across

For the second row: •   Purl 2

•   Purl 2 and knit 2 all the way across

For the third row, which is a decreasing row:

•   Knit 1

•   Slip 1 stitch

•   Knit across until the last three stitches

•   Knit 2 together

•   Knit 1 (up to 48 stitches as rows progress)

For the fourth row, which is an increasing row:

•   Knit 2 stitches

- Make 1 stitch, then knit 2 and make another stitch

- Knit 20 stitches (up to 44 stitches as rows progress)

- Repeat these rows until the piece measures 14 inches.

- Then, you need to create the thumb opening:

- Knit 20

- Bind off 12 stitches

- Knit 20

For the next row:

- Purl 20

- Cast on 2 stitches

- Purl 20 stitches

- Repeat this for 2 more inches, then bind off before sewing the piece together.

Repeat all of this once more for the second glove

Chapter 10 Left-Handed Knitting for Lefties

When it comes to handwork such as knit, left-handers are in no way disadvantaged. Well, maybe except for the fact that most knit instructions are written with right-handers in mind.

While a right-handed knitting will hold the hook with the right hand and use the left hand for the yarn, a left-handed knitting will hold the hook with the left hand and maneuver the yarn with the right hand.

A left-handed knitting can also decide on either the pencil or the knife hold in handling the hook.

In left-handed knit, the knitting follows the same instructions as a right-handed knitting; he/she only needs to work in the opposite direction.

This also means that a right-hander that is reading the instruction for left-handers can also follow the same instructions but work in opposite directions.

How to Knit Left-Handed

Good Knitting Routines

1. Make sure that your hands are clean before picking up your knitting.
2. Always use good lighting for your knitting. A person can make mistakes if the lighting is not good.
3. Sit in a comfortable chair and relax.

4. When tired stop and rest. It is easier to make mistakes when you are tired.

Starting

Knitted items are worked back and forth in rows to make a flat piece. Circular needles are used to work in rounds or can be used to knit flat. A scarf is good for a starter project When you buy yarn for your project buy all that the pattern calls for. Yarn has different dye lots (colors). Make sure that all of the skeins of yarn have all the same dye lot number.

I have found that it is important to take a copy of your project and put it with your knitting, and put a copy of the project with the extra yarn so that you know what the yarn is to be used for. This would be for when you are doing a larger project.

What You Need to Get Started Knitting

You need to save the label on the skein of yarn, because it has all its information on it about the yarn. It tells you, what needle size to use, care instructions, lot number and gauge.

I like to use the yarn from the inside of the skein to start my knitting. To find the beginning of the yarn inside the skein of yarn you need to hold the skein of yarn horizontally in the front of you. Put your index fingers and thumbs into the holes on both ends of the skein.

Remember the Chinese finger-cuffs.

How to Knit Left-Handed

Now wiggle your fingers inside the skein of yarn until your fingers meet. Then feel around on both sides with your fingers to find a small wad of yarn that is loose in the center. Get hold of the wad and pull it gently out one side of the skein. The end for starting use will be inside of this wad of yarn.

Here We Go!

To start with you will need:

1. Light colored yarn (it is easier to see the stitches). Worsted weight yarn is the best to use to learn with. This yarn is easier to work with, when learning to knit. Pick an inexpensive skein of yarn. You should like the color and the feel of the yarn.

2. You need a pair of larger knitting needles. Size US 9 knitting needles are a good starting size.

You can use straight needles or circular needles. Just because the needles are called circular, you can still go back and forth knitting with them. I personal prefer circular needle. The knitting can be pushed back to the middle of the circular needles, and the knitting will not fall off. I find circular needles give me more control and greater range of motion.

When you buy yarn for your project buy all that the pattern calls for. I know I have said this before, but it is important to remember. Yarn has different dye lots (colors) so check to make sure that all of the skeins of yarn have all the same dye lot number.

Cast On

These are the four basic terms of knitting: cast on, knit, purl and cast off Knit= yarn tail is held in back of knitting

Purl= yarn tail is held in front of knitting

It is important to hold the yarn in back for the knit stitch and hold the yarn if the front for the purl stitches.

The stationary needle is the needle in your right hand and the working needle is held in your left hand.

The pattern instructions will tell you to cast on a certain number of stitches. Be sure to place a slip knot on the right needle (the first cast on). Then do the rest of the cast on. This

means putting loops on the needle in your right hand.

1. Make a slip knot about 6 inches from the end of the yarn (the tail end) and loop onto the right-hand needle. This is the needle that is to be held in your right-hand. Pull the yarn tight ---but not too tight. This is for tension, creating the first loop. These loops need to be loose enough for the left needle to be placed inside the loops to make a knit stich.

2. Hold the right needle with the loop in your right hand. You will not need the left needle while you are doing the cast on. Move the loop close to the point of the needle. Make a loop with your left hand. This is done by using the yarn from your skein of yarn. Hold this loop between the thumb and index finger of the left hand, twist it slightly and place it on the right

needle. Tighten the loop so that it holds on the needle without being too snug. You now have two stitches cast on.

3. Continue to make loops and slide them onto the needle until you have as many stitches as you want. Practice your stitches 20 stitches is a decent starting number. This is Your project's first side. Now you can begin to knead the next row.

To Knit a Knit Stitch

The Knit Stitch (along with the Purl Stitch) is one of the foundation stitches for all knitting. All other stitches are simply variations on the Knit or the Purl. The knit stitch forms a

"v" when it is knit.

1. Start by holding the needle with your cast-on stitches in the right hand (the stationary needle), and the other needle in your left hand (the working needle). The needle in your left hand is empty. The yarn that is coming off of the skein of yarn is ALWAYS kept BEHIND your work to make a knit stitch.

2. Now move the stitches up by the point of the needle on the right needle. Slide the left-hand needle into the first loop on the right needle to make sure it goes below the right needle, not to the top. Place the tip of the left needle on the right-hand needle in the first stitch..

The left needle needs to be pointed toward the point of the right needle. Hold the yarn in the back of your work to do a knit stitch. This is done on the front side of the needle. The front side is usually the knit side. The needles form an X shape.

3. Wrap the yarn coming from the skein around the left needle, going from outside the X to the inside. The yarn is now between the two needles. Hold this yarn along the body of the working needle as you use the left needle to pull it back through the loop, which is the first loop on the right-hand needle. Pull the wrapped yarn through the first stitch on the right needle that has the cast on stitches bring the left needle down under and up in front of the right needle. The left needle now holds your first stich. Slide the first loop slowly off of the right needle. Now your first stitch is on your left needle. Keep the yarn between the needles snug, but not too tight. You will need to be able to insert the left needle into the stitches.

4. Keep doing this until you have all of the loops off of the right needle. You have now knit your first row.

5.   To begin the second row, move the needle that is in your left hand that is holding all of the stitches into your right hand. Turn the work so the working end of the right needle is pointed to the left, and repeat the process above. As you keep doing the knit stitch, it will become easier and more relaxing. Try to relax and not keep your knit stitches too tight. You will start to do even stitches. You can do a scarf by doing this knit stitch.

Chapter 11 Tips And Tricks

So, you have decided to join in the fun and crazy world of knitting? Welcome! Fair warning: you will get addicted to this fantastic hobby. It is super fun and at times pretty overwhelming, especially for those just starting out. If you have gone down the knitting aisles at your local craft store staring at the endless rows of yarn and needles, you may be wondering where even to start. Choosing the right supplies to start with will save you tons of time, not to mention save you tons of money. There will be plenty of time to share tips and techniques on how to knit and purl like a professional, but to start you on the path with confidence, this part is geared towards getting you set up with the right supplies and resources for all your future beginning (and some intermediate) projects.

Ten General Tips

1. Do not go overboard in the crafting aisle.

It is beautiful, right? All the fluffy balls of yarn and shiny needles glittering in front of you? Do you envision yourself sitting comfortably, knitting with your beautiful needles, and creating gorgeous gifts? As you wander down the aisle, lightly passing your fingertips over the differently textured wools, you picture all the beautiful crafts you will be making for your friends and family. And before you know it, your cart is full of so many things; you do not remember them hopping into your cart. Several hundred dollars later and crafting room or box overflowing with new toys, it hits you that you have no clue what to start with or what you want to do. Or you start on a project and hate the way aluminum needles feel in your hand, but every time you touch the bamboo needles your friend uses, you swoon. You have a pile of notions you never touch but are always running back to the store to grab just one more of that one thing you use all the time. Save yourself the heartache and hassle, pick up a few of the basics to start, and then add on as you try new techniques or tools.

2. Save your money… in the beginning.

The pretty, sparkly, and colorful yarn is attractive. When it is soft or has a great texture, you just want to run your hands over it again and again. The problem is most of the time that yarn is expensive. As you begin learning, you will be knitting and remove stitches, creating a lot of wear and tear on the yarn. All the pretty glitter and texture will be shredded. Your yarn will tangle—not a fun way to start your knitting experience. You are going to stretch out your first few yarns, so plan on investing in an excellent synthetic yarn that is inexpensive. Save those pretty yarns for when you are more experienced. Part of the joy of your next projects will be running to the store to pick up a flashy, fun, funky ball of yarn and revel in the joy of working with it, preserving the character of the fibers. Test your skills on cheap yarns so you can flex your creative muscles with the pricey ones. Side note: just do not buy the super cheap, acrylic yarn. This does not work well for many projects, especially novice ones. Instead, opt for a natural fiber that is simple.

3. Befriend the basics.

Again, keep your distance from the bedazzled choices of yarn. These are not good starter yarns. Instead, buddy up to the necessary options. Flex your creative muscle with a bold color choice if you have a hard time accepting the simplicity at this point, but try to keep the color light. The important thing is that you see your stitches as you practice, and a lighter yarn color will make it more apparent when you miss a stitch or make a mistake. Worsted weight wool is one of the most basic options you can go with.

4. Get curious about new ideas.

The beauty of knitting today is that there is a plethora of techniques and options out there for you to experiment with. As you are learning, now is a great time to try out some fun ideas. When you are following a pattern and it throws a challenge at you, give it a shot. Directions for cables and yarns over may scare you at first, but when you get into them, you will find they are not that bad. Plus, did you start knitting for just simple scarves? Probably not! So, this is the time to conquer your fear of a decrease and knit those beautiful hats!

5. Search for inspiration and enjoy the creativity.

Scour Pinterest, stalk knitting blogs, browse images of knitted projects to become inspired with what you will knit one day. Think about expanding your repertoire of knitting projects to include headbands, gloves, and other fun "newbie" projects. Many sites will allow you to search their pattern database by skill level so you can find projects that you can complete at this stage and droll over projects that you want to challenge yourself with as you keep practicing. This not only helps you find new projects but when frustration and boredom kick in, you can scroll through your favorite places to reignite the dream you have of becoming a glorious knitter.

6. Use your resources.

There are plenty of resources out there that you can use to get started and to help you advance. This book is one of them! Use it. If you are getting frustrated with something, check out the pages of this book for tips on how to accomplish it or spend a few minutes on YouTube watching a video to nail that purl. You do not need to suffer alone. This and other resources are out there to get you to where you want to be. All else fails? Throw it in a bag and take it into your local yarn shop and get some advice! Maybe join a knitting group in the area so you have a community of knitters to help you learn the tricks of the trade.

7. Put it away before someone (or something) gets hurt!

You have knitted and removed stitches for what feels like hours and are still not past the first row of stitches. You just want to throw it at the TV and cry. Take a deep breath—this has happened (and often still does) to all of us. Put your knitting aside, take a little (or a lot) time to yourself, and then go back at it again when you are ready. If you try to power through the frustration, you will probably contract "crazy knitter fit" and will infect your project with it. You will get so annoyed with the one slipped stitch that you will keep making the same mistake throughout the project, and it almost never ends well. Coming at the problem with calm and rested eyes will often help you solve the problem, at least easier than before, and get you moving again.

8. Know your abbreviations or at least have a cheat sheet handy.

As you progress in your knitting career, you will probably move on to patterns. Many of your patterns will explain the abbreviations they use, but some will not. If you do not have much experience with knitting patterns, it may look like gibberish to you. This is a simple fix: keep a list of abbreviations and a short description of what they are. Add new terms and stitches to the list as you go. Stash this list in your knitting supplies so you can add or reference it as you are working. You will be surprised how this will make your life so much easier.

9. Hold on to your practice projects.

As you are learning, you will have plenty of projects that just do not turn out showcase-worthy. That is normal and actually a good thing. But instead of tossing those practice projects, consider taking them apart to reuse the yarn for another project or using parts of them in a new craft if there are salvageable pieces. Upcycle or recycle these projects later as you become more skilled. Even when you are a knitter either intermediate or advanced, you will have practice projects, and learning this tip now will save you a lot of time and money in the long run.

10. Relax! This is supposed to be fun.

Knitting can be relaxing and fun, or you could let it stress you out and cause anxiety. You should choose knitting for the latter. So, what if you mess up? Laugh it off! Knitting takes time and practice, so the more you learn from it, the better you will get. Enjoy the ride. You can take this with you anywhere, you can lose yourself in the repetition, and you can challenge yourself with new ideas. Venture out and try it;

Chapter 12 Common Mistakes

Place pens look like such a headache. Significant and also dangly ones enter your way. Tiny ones might not glide smoothly on big needles. They all take some time to put on the needles and also make extra effort to relocate them while weaving stitches. After that, why utilize them? They form a pointer while you knit.

From basic garter stitch to demanding shoelace, the stitch pens tell a knitter that something happens with specific requirements. A marker says, "Oh, take note here" when switching to a different thread, a brand-new stitch, or pattern repeat.

If you are knitting for the first time, familiarize yourself with the methods, the stitches, the feel of the yarn, and more. Utilizing a pen provides a starting up knitter with the fact, back still to considering the pattern to determine what comes subsequently, even directly back to putting those last couple of stitches on develop a beautiful boundary.

When I just started knitting, I made the common mistake of not making use of pens. I assumed that as long as I adhered to the pattern, every little thing would work out great. Well, it didn't. If the design called for the same kind of stitch in the model, however, various one for the boundary, I occasionally kept knitting the pattern stitch to the end of the row.

My mistakes didn't appear until I weaved even more rows a whole lot. Since I had not yet learned how to undo stitches without removing rows, I had to choose between eliminating several rows or leaving the error in object. I found the errors in certain situations just to hinder the piece way too late after that.

Correctly how to Fix It

If the pattern does not call for pens to be put, there's no reason you shouldn't work without them. Attempt to place pens at the beginning or end of pattern repeats, right after or right before a border line, at a sign up with when knitting in the circle, or at a change of color for knitting Fair Isle. All good choices and up to you to choose which ones work best for you.

Sew markers perform equally well for counting rows for a job of lots of rows. Using a contrasting piece of cotton yarn or yarn that won't leave little bits and pieces of fiber behind as it is clear. Take a small part, tie a knot, and slip it over your needle before a row is complete. Knit a set of rows, like 5 or 10, and then add another marker. Clip out when all is set for obstructing your completed job.

If you forget to add a needle with cotton yarn to these little markers, thread it and run it carefully with a stitch. Create a string knot, and you have another pad. The pens which open and close make an additional great choice to keep track of rows. This could be used during or after kneading the lines.

Picking the incorrect Cast-On

Externally, every cast-on does the same thing by creating loops on a needle that obtain sweated off by drawing yarn through them with a 2nd needle. However, a standard knitting error made by several beginners can be to choose the incorrect cast-on for a task or to alter the cast-on recommended by the pattern developer.

Each type of cast-on has a function beyond developing those first loops. A cast-on sets the phase for the garment. For instance, when casting-on stitches for the leg opening of a sock, the wrong cast-on can make it a fight to obtain the hose on over your foot or worse, it can trigger a fall around your ankles.

Cast-on either offers the edge of your job both stretch as well as elasticity or just sufficient stretch for putting on while sustaining the continuing to be stitched in the garment. When you make use of an elastic cast-on, such as a weaved cast-on, the edge of your project will relocate conveniently. Nonetheless, if you utilize this type of cast-on for something like the neck of a gown that you wish to lie level, it may not support the stitches in the corset, causing it to gap open rather than exist flat against your skin.

The Fix

If a pattern does not state which cast-on to use, numerous knowledgeable knitters use the long-tail cast-on as their go-to cast-on. Moderately stretchy with a tip of the framework, the long tail-cast on helps a lot of jobs

If the cast-on looks too limited, removing and beginning again with a different one may be your best option. Believe me. I've done this more frequently than I like to confess, but obtaining the cast-on right makes the rest of the project job far better.

If the builder selected a particular cast-on, however, your cast-on side features too much overall flexibility, try out casting-on with an inferior sized needle, then proceed to the needle required in the pattern to start your very first row. Alternatively, if the cast-on has excessive structure, cast-on with a bigger sized needle, then move to the appropriate size for the very first row.

If the job has way too much elasticity at the cast-on edge, usage progressed, finishing methods to add definition to the side.

Binding Off Too Tightly

The tension utilized when binding off helps give form to your job. When you bind off stitches as well snugly, some points take place.

It makes it impossible for you to obtain perfect measurements, normally impossible since a restricted bind off squeezes your stitches towards the biggest market of the job.

Your cast-on for a toe-up sock might be excellent, however, if you bind off also tightly for the leg opening, good luck obtaining that sock over your ankle joint. The same point occurs for neck or wrist openings.

It makes an inflexible straight side that doesn't feel or look good, which frequently contrasts with the soft qualities of the rest of the task.

If you normally knead with tighter tension, switch your stitches to a 1 to 2-dimensional needle that is more important than the one used for the job. Bind off with needles bigger scale.

If you usually maintain tension when knitting by wrapping the working yarn around your fingers, drop it down for the bind off. Instead, the working yarn is spread loosely over one finger or between 2 fingers for stitch catch. Enable the yarn to pass over your fingers or between them to stay clear of the extra tension.

If you knit within the American or United Kingdom style, hold the yarn in the middle of your fingers as well as cover it freely around the needle to make the bind off stitch without drawing it as tight as you would certainly for a typical knit or purl sew.

Most importantly, check the tension after the last stitch binding off as well as before raising the yarn. If it still looks closely, unpick the stitches completely, place the stitches back on a needle, and reshape the bind off. Yeah, I did it, too.

Selecting the Wrong Yarn for a Project

Whether knitting from your very own design or from a pattern created by somebody else, choosing the right yarn for the task helps ensure the garment turns out lovely.

In some cases, you do intend to see if a dimension 80 tatting cotton thread knits the like gossamer Shetland. And that's a high point to do since testing when knitting creates enjoyable times. Nevertheless, using the ideal yarn does have an objective and also recognizing exactly how different threads curtain, lose, knit-up, tablet, and more make a distinction. Besides, yarn weight and color contribute to the yarn option.

When a coat pattern needs a DK weight merino wool as well as choosing a fingering weight alpaca, the thickness will not only be off, but the arms, as well as the jacket, will pool at the wrists as well as the middle part respectively, as the soft fibers of alpaca drape higher than the wool. You may want the presence, but if not, why was the effort wasted?

Changing the fiber also impacts the garment. The majority of pet fibers have a halo, with mohair and angora revealing the most corona. These fuzzy tendrils of texture include extra warmth to a weaved garment. When selecting them for a shoelace task, the halo hides a lot of the pattern.

Chapter 13 FAQ

1. Why is knitting a good skill to have?

Knitting is a brilliantly useful skill that can help you create a wide variety of your own products – everything from toys to clothing. But, not only that, it's scientifically proven to improve your mood, mind and body. It's a therapeutic skill which you will not regret learning!

2. How do you read a knitting chart?

The best way to read a knitting chart is explained in detail in this guide, in the Knitting Charts.

3. What I need to buy to start off knitting?

The Supplies part of this guide gives you the basics of what you need to start knitting. However, the yarns, needles and anything extra you'll need for a specific pattern will be listed as one of the first pieces of information.

4. How do you do double-pointed knitting?

Double pointed needles are generally used for knitting in the round on projects that are too small for circular needles. They are often purchased in sets of 5. Here is a brilliant guide for how to use them, with these main top tips:

• Cast on to 1 double pointed needle.

• Then slip ½ the stitches onto another needle.

- Then a third onto another.

- Use a fourth needle to knit.

See How to Knit With Double Pointed Needles In Round

5. Does it cost a lot to knit?

Knitting can be done very cheaply if you know the right places to look. Local haberdashery stores will sell a wide range of products from high quality to budget so it really is a skill that applies to everyone.

6. What is an easy way to learn how to knit?

The step-by-step guides provided in the Stitches part of this guide will get you started. If you need extra help, check out some of the online Sources provided.

7. What is the Garter stitch in knitting?

A brilliant guide to completing the Garter Stitch can be found here.

8. How do you knit with 3 needles?

You will often use 3 or more needles when working with double pointed needles. This has been explained here.

9. What are the differences for English and continental methods for knitting?

Everyone has their own preference when it comes to knitting style. You will eventually develop your own.

English Knitting

- Hold yarn in right hand
- Throw yarn when wrapping
- Easier with chunky weight yarns
- Continental Knitting
- Hold yarn in left hand
- Pick the yarn when wrapping
- Faster when you're knitting the knit stitch
- Alternating stitches is easier
- Easier for crocheters to learn

Watch Continental vs. English Style Knitting

10. Where can I find stretch knit fabric?

Your local haberdashery store will sell all sorts of fabrics, including stretch knit. There will also be many online resources, such as here.

11. What is knitting in tandem?

Tandem knitting is a technique for knitting socks or gloves or anything in the round that comes in pairs and uses 9 DPNs, it casts on for both items in the pair at the same time, and involves completing a portion of one of the pair, then the same portion of the other item of the pair.

12. Is it hard to knit a scarf?

In the Patterns part of this guide, you will find a pattern for a knitted scarf designed specifically for beginners. Scarves can be made by anyone at any skill level. If you're an advanced knitter, your creations can be much more complex and embellished.

13. Is crocheting harder than knitting?

Crocheting is a different skill to knitting in the way that it uses one hook rather than two needles. Different people prefer different skills so practicing both is the best way to figure out which one you personally find easier and more suitable.

14. Where can I find some great knitting patterns?

Knitting patterns can be found in haberdashery stores, but they are also available in abundance online. Just type 'Knitting Patterns' into any search engine and you will be spoilt for choice.

15. What are the next steps once you've worked through this guide?

This book gives you all the basics you need for starting knitting. Once you have gotten to grips with all of the stitches and patterns provided, it is time to move on to more complex patterns – you can maybe even create your own! Once you have mastered this skill, the possibilities are endless.

Conclusion

Thank you for making it to the end. Knitting is the process of creating thread loops which interlock row by row, using yarns and needles. Many have used this art to make fabrics and garments such as boots, sweaters, scarves, caps, and skirts. In the 15th century, the word knit was only mentioned in the Oxford Unabridged English Dictionary. It came from the word crystal, meaning to tie with a knot. However, in modern English, this verb has several examples. They also use the term to combine or draw together in describing the verbs.

Always remember knitting can be done by you or in a standard way. It doesn't require a lot of space as you'll need only a pair of needles and a yarn to build your art. It has been widely practiced nowadays as a type of therapeutic activity or as a hobby. Numerous knitting clubs and organizations such as Makers Mercantile and Ravelry are being set up to serve people in this form of art with passionate passion and enthusiasm. Some have still been questioning the legendary roots of the knitting art. No-one has ever known the exact date when a knitted object was first made. Knitting, however, is said to originate in the Middle East and is recognized among spinning and weaving as the youngest craft. The old knitted garments were made from natural fibers such as cotton, wool, and silk. These materials quickly decompose, which rendered tracking the period when this practice occurred even more difficult. We also mentioned the history of knitting in this article-from the ancient times to the present.

So, let's first find out and learn more about the wonders and mysteries in the world of knitting, before picking those yarns and needles.

In the fashion world, knitwear, such as sweaters and pullovers, played an essential part. It became a fashion statement for men and women of all ages and was synonymous with sports and leisure activities such as golf, tennis, and cricket. Even Coco Chanel promoted this craft and made widespread use of such objects and patterns. The popularity of knitting continued its trajectory on the great depression but altered its direction as a means of need. Since producing your garments was much cheaper, people preferred to make their own instead of purchasing the commercial products. In boycott British products, the people knead their clothes, demonstrating their self-reliance and freedom from the British. Martha Washington, the wife of George Washington, is a committed knitter too. She called the wives of the colonial army's high-ranking officials to knit and mend garments like socks and uniforms for the troops. Many cities, such as Nottingham, have become a leading producer of machine-knitted fabrics. Leicestershire's land and some of its neighboring countries have expanded into the hosiery or legwear market.

Despite the fact that you might need to hop directly in there and begin utilizing a knitting pattern it is a smart thought to make a check swatch. Try not to skirt this progression, you will be grieved and it's not justified, despite any potential benefits. A large portion of a line in one inch can wind up having a major effect to the general size of a sweater. Continuously weave the swatch in the join that you will utilize. Clearly different knitting patterns end up with different sizes so this issues. I generally attempt to make my swatch sufficiently large to make it a decent test. I generally go for at any rate 4" x 4". Encompass the swatch with a couple of columns of seed fasten knitting (weave or purl the contrary line of what you see confronting you on odd number lines). Start and end each line with four seed lines also. This join lies exceptionally level and will assist you with estimating precisely.

One of the great things about knitting is that you can create a wide range of items with the same simple steps. Only choose a different yarn form, and a different stitch variation and a very different final product can be made.

Archeologists have been able to find evidence of knitting since the first millennium. Knitting has certainly been around for a long time. Even the ancient Egyptians knead bright socks and other accessories. It is generally thought that the first people to knit were ancient Arabs, who made clothes and shoes.

The best thing for knitters is to join a knitting circle. In a circle of knitting, the members meet with their yarn and needles at different members ' homes or the local coffee shop.

If you are alone, you can always turn for a wealth of knitting resources to the Internet. Groups, forums, and message boards offer communication tools for knitters to put them together.

Best of luck!